The Duckl... Monster

Story by Stephen Thraves

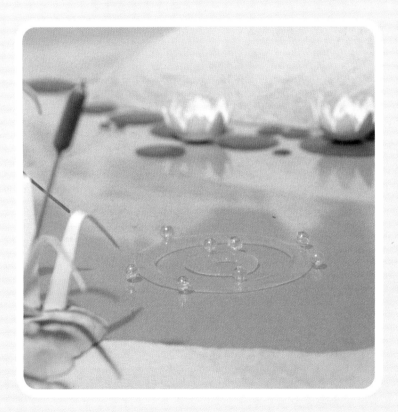

Based on the TV series, Fetch the Vet

Little Hippo

With thanks for technical help:
Suzanne Whight BVSc MRCVS
(Greenwood Veterinary Clinic, Chalfont St Peter)

Scholastic Children's Books,
Commonwealth House, 1-19 New Oxford Street,
London WC1A 1NU, UK
a division of Scholastic Ltd

London ~ New York ~ Toronto ~ Sydney ~ Auckland
Mexico City ~ New Delhi ~ Hong Kong

First published in the UK by Scholastic Ltd, 2001

Based upon the television series FETCH THE VET produced
by Flextech Rights Ltd and ITEL in association with Cosgrove Hall Films.
Original concept by Stephen Thraves and Gail Penston.

Text copyright © Stephen Thraves, 2001
Illustrations derived from FETCH THE VET television series,
copyright © Flextech Rights Ltd and ITEL, 2001.
Photographs by Jean-Marc Ferriere and Justin Nöe

ISBN 0 439 99331 8

Printed in Spain
by Artes Gráficas Toledo S.A.U.
D.L. TO: 62-2001

Tom Fetch the vet had just finished his morning surgery and was saying goodbye to Kara.

Today was an important day for Duckhurst. The judges for the Best Kept Village Competition were visiting and it was Kara's job to make sure everywhere looked very smart.

Kara's first stop was the pet shop and she was pleased to see that Lionel Froggatt was busy washing his windows.

"I've never seen them look so clean, Lionel!" she told him.

"But they're not clean at all, Kara," he grumbled. "I keep rubbing and rubbing but I just don't seem to be able to get the soap off!"

Kara chuckled, "That's because you've got the soap all over your glasses!"

Kara noticed a strange gold box near the door. It was the ugliest box she had ever seen!

Lionel told her that it had just been delivered to his shop. "It's a luxury cat carrier," he said. "Violet Blush asked me to order it for her."

"Violet Blush! I might have known!" Kara exclaimed. "Well, please make sure you hide it before the judges arrive!" she laughed.

Lionel had just taken the cat carrier into his shop when he heard someone parking noisily outside. It could only be Violet Blush.

"Quick, Iggy!" he said to his pet iguana. "You had better go upstairs and hide in my bedroom!"

Lionel knew that Violet did not like Iggy very much!

Iggy scampered off just before Violet came bursting into the shop.

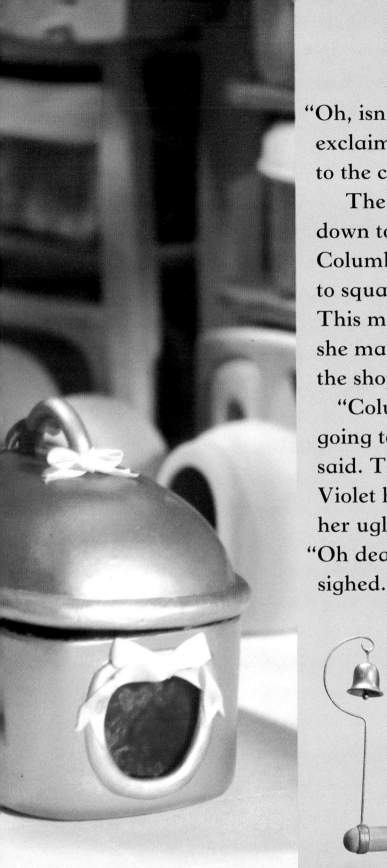

"Oh, isn't it beautiful!" Violet exclaimed as she marched up to the cat carrier.

The moment she knelt down to inspect it, however, Columbus the parrot started to squawk rude names at her. This made Violet so cross that she marched straight out of the shop again.

"Columbus! Whatever am I going to do with you?" Lionel said. Then he noticed that Violet had forgotten to take her ugly cat carrier with her. "Oh dear! Oh dear!" he sighed.

On the village green, Pippa and Lucy were playing happily on the swings.

Joe suddenly arrived, showing them a video he had just borrowed.

"It's all about a terrifying monster that lives in a muddy lake!" he told them with a huge grin.

Joe walked with the girls to the duck pond. He decided to try to scare them!

"Look!" he gasped suddenly. "There's a monster hiding in Duckhurst pond too. You can just see its head and neck sticking out of the water!"

Lucy was really frightened but Pippa just laughed. "Joe's only being silly!" she told Lucy. "It's just an old Wellington boot!"

As Joe and Pippa were walking away from the pond, they heard a shriek.

It was Lucy. She told them she had screamed because there really was a monster in the pond. At first, Pippa and Joe thought she was just pretending but then they saw lots of bubbles appear in the water. And they just glimpsed the top of a green wrinkly head!

The children decided there was only one thing to do – fetch the vet!

"Mr Fetch will know whether it's a monster or not," Pippa said.

Fetch hurried with the children back to the pond.

"A green wrinkly head you say?" he asked, looking very puzzled. "Are you sure it wasn't just a frog?"

But Joe said, "It was much bigger than a frog. Much, MUCH bigger!"

When they reached the pond, Fetch could see no sign of the monster. He was beginning to wonder if the children were just playing a joke on him.

Then lots of bubbles appeared on the pond and he too suddenly glimpsed a green wrinkly head!

Just then Lionel arrived, panting heavily. He was very upset.

Lionel told them that Iggy had crawled out of his bedroom window and escaped from the pet shop. He couldn't find him anywhere!

At that moment, the bubbles suddenly appeared again on the pond. The green wrinkly head suddenly popped up again too!

This time the creature came right out of the water, crawling on to a little island in the middle of the pond.

"It's Iggy!" Lionel exclaimed with joy. "So this is where he ran off to!"

Fetch and the children were delighted to find that the Duckhurst Monster was just Iggy.

But as she turned round, Pippa suddenly gasped.

"Oh no!" she exclaimed. "There's Kara with the judges for the Best Kept Village Competition. They're heading right this way!"

Pippa was worried that if the judges saw Iggy in the pond, Duckhurst would not win the Best Kept Village Competition.

"We must try to lure Iggy to the edge somehow," Fetch said, thinking hard. He told Joe to signal to Kara and secretly let her know that she must try to delay the judges.

Fetch suddenly had a brilliant idea. He took one of his carrots from his pocket and held it out towards Iggy.

Iggy loved carrots and so he immediately crawled off the island and swam towards Fetch.

At least Iggy was now out of the pond but how were they going to lead him away without the judges seeing him?

It was now Lionel's turn to have a brilliant idea. "I've got just the answer!" he said and he immediately ran off towards his shop.

Lionel collected Violet's special cat carrier from his shop.

He hurried back with it to the pond and with Fetch's help, he carefully placed Iggy inside. By the time Kara and the judges arrived at the pond, Iggy was nowhere to be seen.

"What a lovely village pond!" one of the judges declared, not realising Iggy was only centimetres away. "So quiet and peaceful!"

Fetch and the children carried Iggy away in the ugly box
right under the judges' noses.

"That was a close shave, everyone!" chuckled Fetch as
they all returned to his clinic.

Soon afterwards Kara and Violet walked in, holding
a huge trophy. Duckhurst had won the Best Kept Village
Competition!

"All thanks to Violet's wonderful cat carrier!"
Fetch laughed.